Poverty

Clive Gifford

Evans

TITLES IN THE VOICES SERIES:

**AIDS • CHILD LABOUR • DRUGS ON THE STREET • GANGS
HUNGER • POVERTY • RACE HATE • RELIGIOUS EXTREMISM
VIOLENCE • VIOLENCE ON THE SCREEN • WAR**

Published by Evans Brothers Limited
2A Portman Mansions
Chiltern Street
London W1U 6NR

First published 2009
© copyright Evans Brothers 2009

VISIT OUR WEBSITE
www.evansbooks.co.uk
Evans

Produced for Evans Brothers Limited by
Monkey Puzzle Media Ltd
Little Manor Farm, The Street
Brundish, Woodbridge
Suffolk IP13 8BL, UK

British Library Cataloguing in Publication Data
Gifford, Clive
Poverty. – (Voices)
1. Poverty – Juvenile literature
I. Title
362.5

ISBN-13: 978 0 237 53720 3

Editor: Susie Brooks
Designer: Mayer Media Ltd
Picture research: Susie Brooks and Lynda Lines
Graphs and charts: Martin Darlison, Encompass Graphics

Picture acknowledgements
Photographs were kindly supplied by the following:
Alamy 37 (vario images GmbH & Co.KG); Corbis 6
(Les Stone/Sygma), 27 (Janet Jarman), 28 (Collart
Hervé/Sygma), 32 (Karen Kasmauski), 34 (Sherwin
Crasto/Reuters); Getty Images front cover, 14, 16 (AFP),
18 (National Geographic), 19 (AFP), 20 (Ian Shaw), 26
(Christopher Pillitz), 29, 31, 35 (AFP), 38, 40 (AFP);
Panos Pictures 1 (Zed Nelson), 8 (Karen Robinson),
10 (Paul Lowe), 13 (Martin Roemers), 15 (Zed Nelson),
17 (Alayung Thaksin), 22 (Robert Wallis), 33 (Dieter
Telemans), 39 (Martin Roemers), 42–43 (Zed Nelson),
45 (Paul Lowe); Photolibrary.com 12 (Aurora); Rex
Features 36 (Sipa); Still Pictures 41 Jean-Léo Dugast);
Topfoto.co.uk 7 (Prisma/VWpics), 24 (ImageWorks).

Cover picture: A homeless man carries his belongings
to a shelter in Boston, USA.

CONTENTS

WHAT IS POVERTY?

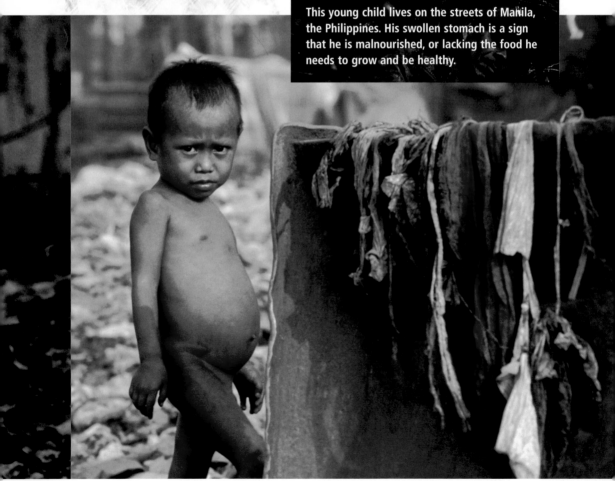

Poverty is what people experience when they lack the basic things they need to live. You might feel poor when you can't afford new DVDs or computer games. But imagine if food, water and medical care were out of reach.

A constant struggle

The United Nations (UN) estimates that more than a billion people around the world struggle to find food, clean water and safe shelter. They are suffering severe poverty, like these children living rough in the Philippines:

❝ We are poor. We know that because we are not able to eat three times a day, we don't go to school and we don't have clothes. We can't buy things like a TV or radio, and we live in a squatter area. ❞

This young child lives on the streets of Manila, the Philippines. His swollen stomach is a sign that he is malnourished, or lacking the food he needs to grow and be healthy.

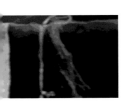

THE WORLD'S POOR CHILDREN

- Over 500 million children live with no toilet facility.
- 376 million children use unsafe water sources or have to walk more than 15 minutes for water.
- 134 million children aged 7–18 have never been to school.
- 91 million children are severely malnourished.

UNICEF Child Poverty In The Developing World, 2004

Poverty can strike people of all ages, but the youngest and oldest members of society are often most at risk. This older man is begging for money to survive.

Hungry, sick and helpless

Poverty is a huge challenge because it causes other very serious problems. It leads to starvation, disease and death on a massive scale. Being poor can also hurt people emotionally, making them feel scared and helpless. A blind woman from Tiraspol, in Moldova, explains:

❝ For a poor person everything is terrible – illness, humiliation, shame. We are cripples; we are afraid of everything; we depend on everyone. No one needs us. We are like garbage that everyone wants to get rid of. ❞

"Poverty devastates families, communities and nations. It causes instability and political unrest and fuels conflict."
Kofi Annan, former United Nations Secretary-General, 2005.

HOW IS POVERTY MEASURED?

Poverty is a complex issue and is measured in a number of different ways. How do people decide who is truly poor?

This household in Birmingham is poor compared to others in the UK. Yet families like this still have more resources than the poor in many other parts of the world.

Relative poverty

Relative poverty compares someone's money and possessions to others in the same society, country or region. This clearly shows whose income falls below the national average. But it does not help to compare people all over the world. Ananh, a college student in Laos, feels it misses the full picture:

" Hearing about poor people in America makes me laugh. They are not truly poor, they all eat. Someone who earned £5,000 a year would be below the poverty line in the UK or America. But in other, poorer countries like my own, they would be comfortable, wealthy even. "

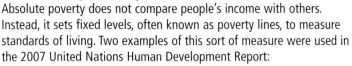

Absolute poverty

Absolute poverty does not compare people's income with others. Instead, it sets fixed levels, often known as poverty lines, to measure standards of living. Two examples of this sort of measure were used in the 2007 United Nations Human Development Report:

❝ There are still around 1 billion people living at the margins of survival on less than US$1 a day, with 2.6 billion – 40 per cent of the world's population – living on less than US$2 a day. ❞

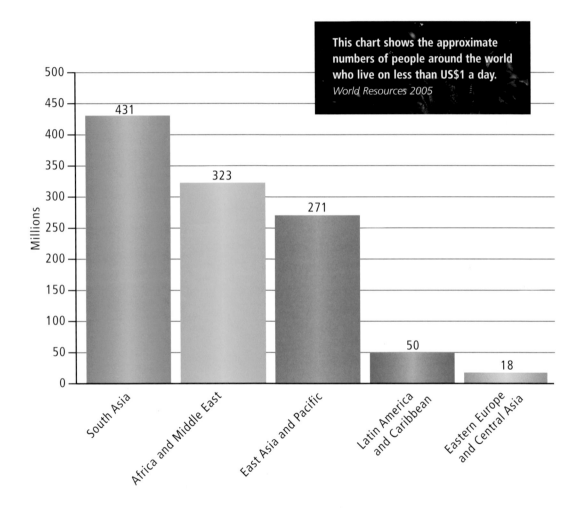

This chart shows the approximate numbers of people around the world who live on less than US$1 a day.
World Resources 2005

"A person is considered poor if his or her income level falls below some minimum level necessary to meet basic needs. This minimum level is usually called the 'poverty line'. What is necessary to satisfy basic needs varies across time and societies. Therefore, poverty lines vary in time and place."
The World Bank.

WHAT IS EXTREME POVERTY LIKE?

People in extreme poverty face a daily fight for survival. They can rarely afford enough to eat, basic healthcare, shelter or schooling. As a result, they have few opportunities to improve their lives.

Always hungry

Millions of the world's poorest people go hungry every day. Many develop severe malnutrition, which means their bodies do not get the nutrients they need to grow and be healthy. Malnourished people are more likely to fall ill and die younger. Ten-year-old 'J' in Gabon, Africa, fears this could happen to him:

❝ When I leave for school in the mornings I don't have any breakfast. At noon there is no lunch. In the evening I get a little supper, and that is not enough. So when I see another child eating, I watch him, and if he doesn't give me something I think I'm going to die of hunger. ❞

Many African countries suffer from droughts, famines and extreme poverty. These painfully thin Dinka people are from southern Sudan, where thousands have died of starvation.

Unsafe and ill

People in extreme poverty are very vulnerable. As well as being hungry and weak, they have little security and are easily robbed or attacked. Many extreme poor are forced to drink unsafe water, which can cause deadly illnesses. Kali is a child in rural India who does not know the luxury of turning on a tap at home:

❝ There is a clean water well, but it is an hour away and is often guarded by thugs who will beat you and steal your clothes. The water nearby is brown and full of insects. My two best friends are dead from diarrhoeal disease. I fear I will be next. ❞

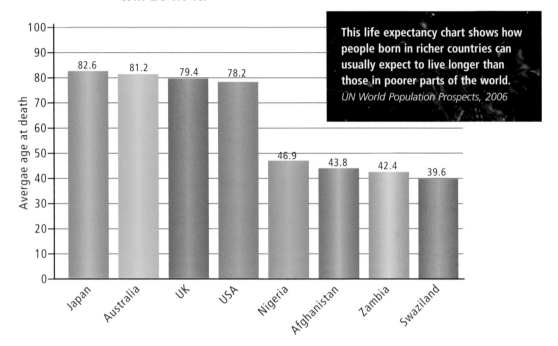

This life expectancy chart shows how people born in richer countries can usually expect to live longer than those in poorer parts of the world.
UN World Population Prospects, 2006

Bar chart — Average age at death:
- Japan: 82.6
- Australia: 81.2
- UK: 79.4
- USA: 78.2
- Nigeria: 46.9
- Afghanistan: 43.8
- Zambia: 42.4
- Swaziland: 39.6

"Poor water quality continues to pose a major threat to human health. Diarrhoeal disease [caused by using unsafe water] is responsible for the deaths of 1.8 million people every year."
World Health Organisation, 2008.

DYING OF POVERTY

Every day, more than 26,000 children die. Two out of three child deaths in Africa and South-east Asia are due to just six diseases – tuberculosis, malaria, HIV/AIDS, measles, pneumonia and diarrhoea. Many of these could be prevented with the right healthcare.

American Council for Voluntary International Action

DOES POVERTY OCCUR ONLY IN POOR COUNTRIES?

Poverty is widespread in the developing world, where countries are still trying to build their economies. But are there poor people in wealthy, developed countries too?

Poor and poorer

There are millions of poor people in wealthy countries, though very few suffer the extreme poverty that exists in the developing world. Elias was 13 when his family moved from Germany to a poor town in Nepal. He wasn't prepared for the food shortages, disease and unclean water he found there:

❝ The change from my convenient life in Germany was quite a shock to me. And still, I realised that we were far better off than the people suffering on the streets. That was difficult for me. When I talk about poverty now, I always think about these people in Nepal. ❞

Sprawling slums like these in India are a familiar sight in poor countries, but not in the developed world. These children are walking along a pipeline that supplies richer parts of the city with water.

Poor in a wealthy land

Being poor in a wealthy country may be less extreme – but does that make it any easier? Juana lives with her mother and three brothers in a single-room apartment in the USA. She lists some of the worst things about being poor in a rich nation:

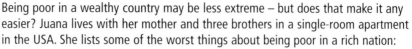

❝ Sleeping three in a bed, having no toilet, the terrible looks you get, not getting served even when you have money, not being able to do things other kids do, going to bed having eaten nothing all day, watching TV and seeing how everyone except us lives well. ❞

"Although poverty here is different to that in developing countries, its causes and impact can be very similar. That's why we set up the UK Poverty Programme in 1996, to give people a voice."
Oxfam UK, 2008.

A poverty-stricken homeless man is moved on by police officers in one of the world's wealthiest cities, New York.

INFANT MORTALITY

Infant mortality is the number of babies born who die before their first birthday. It can be a measure of poverty, as these figures show:

World (2001): infant mortality on average 8 times higher in the developing world than in developed countries.

UK (2005): infant mortality 19% higher for poorer families than the rest of the population.

USA (2006): infant mortality rate rising due to rising poverty.

UN World Population Prospects database, 2006

HOW DO PEOPLE GET TRAPPED IN POVERTY?

People can become poor in many different ways. Some are thrown into poverty suddenly. Others are made poor over years of unfairness or problems in a region. Many people are born into poverty and find they can't escape.

Like thousands of others, this New Orleans family was left homeless, jobless and in financial trouble after Hurricane Katrina devastated the southern USA in 2005.

Sudden disaster

People who work hard to earn a living can find themselves suddenly struggling to make ends meet. This may be due to conflict in their area or country, a natural disaster or problems in the economy. Pini describes what happened to her family in a small rural village in southern Italy:

❝ The one factory in our village closed. My mother and father both worked there and now there is no work in the village. We have gone from being well-off to being poor. My father sold our car. We walk everywhere now or take the bus. Life is hard and it is not our fault. ❞

Born poor, die poor

Millions of people are born extremely poor and may never know anything else. Escaping poverty is very difficult when you can't afford to go to school. Some 781 million adults – one in five in the world – cannot read or write. Gurinda, an Indian girl, says this is a problem for her parents:

❝ My father never gets work because he cannot read. He says girls don't need to learn and I cannot get to a school. No one cares, we are left to rot. I don't want to grow up like this with mud for a floor and being afraid of the next day. ❞

A Bangladeshi mother works for little pay at a local brick factory. For many people trapped in low-paid jobs, escaping from poverty seems impossible.

"Those that grow up in poverty are more likely to have learning difficulties, to drop out of school, to resort to drugs, to commit crimes, to be out of work and to live lives that perpetuate [continue] poverty and disadvantage into succeeding generations."
Innocenti Research Centre, 2000.

IS BAD GOVERNMENT TO BLAME?

Governments have to make many decisions and are often blamed when they get these wrong. Is bad government to blame for poverty?

Corrupt and careless

Some governments are corrupt. They take money and aid that is meant for the poor, and use it for themselves and their supporters. Sifatullah is a doctor working in Kabul, Afghanistan. He worries about his country's leadership:

❝ There is so much aid money pouring into our country from international donors, but where is it being spent? It seems to disappear in corrupt deals which do nothing to help the poor. Water is sold to irrigate neighbouring countries and no investment is made in agriculture here... electricity is bought from outside the country when there are 20 dams here already. ❞

Robert Mugabe has governed Zimbabwe for over 25 years. Recently his country has suffered terribly from mass unemployment, extreme poverty and human rights abuses.

"Corrupt politicians squander public resources on uneconomic 'trophy' projects like dams, power plants, and refineries, at the expense of less spectacular but more necessary projects like schools, roads, or the supply of power and water to rural areas."
John O'Shea, founder of aid agency GOAL.

Out of their control?

Some causes of poverty may be out of a government's control. Many people feel that their leaders can't do much about events such as changes in the world economy or natural disasters. Ahmed, a teenager from the flood-torn district of Noakhali in Bangladesh, is one of them:

❝ Our government may not be perfect, but what can it do to control the floods that wiped out my family's crops and the crops of thousands more? How can it stop earthquakes or droughts, or fight for a better deal against richer and more powerful countries? ❞

Villagers await help in Myanmar, 2008, after a severe cyclone destroyed their homes. The government could not prevent the disaster, but it was responsible for long delays in getting aid to its people.

SHOULD WE CANCEL POOR COUNTRIES' DEBTS?

More than 50 developing countries, most in Africa, are in debt to wealthier nations who have loaned them money in the past. Should these debts be cancelled to give the poor a chance?

Debt duty

In 2003, Nigeria repaid debts of US$1,600 million. This was more than its total spending on both healthcare and education. Many people feel that poor countries should be allowed to keep the money they have borrowed, to help reduce their poverty. Francis, from Kigali in Rwanda, says the rich nations have a duty to the poorest because they exploited them in the past:

" For centuries, the West plundered resources on the African continent until there was nothing left for the Africans. The West can help by completely writing off the debt owed by African countries and bringing in lots of investments. "

The cancellation of some of Tanzania's debts in 2006 led to dozens of new schools being built there.

"What poor countries in Africa spend on debt repayments each year could save the lives of 3 million children."

UN Human Development Report.

In 2007, Ghana spent around US$20 million celebrating its 50th year of independence, while 40 per cent of Ghanaians live on less than US$1 per day. Would debt cancellation really help those who need it most?

CANCELLING DEBTS

Some debt cancellation is already happening. Up to 2007:

● Debt cancellation total: US$83,000 million

● Number of countries: 23

● Average increase in education spending [in these countries]: 40%

● Average increase in health spending: 70%

Jubilee Debt Campaign, 2008

Whose responsibility?

Some people wonder if cancelling debt is the right thing. Will it send out a message that corrupt governments can get away with spending even more? Michel, a teenager from Marseilles in France, fears so:

❝ Many of the countries we're told are most in debt are still buying new weapons, fighting unnecessary wars or spending on crazy schemes not on the poor. Those countries took and spent the money. If they decide it isn't their responsibility to pay, who would ever lend them money for important projects in the future? ❞

DO RICH COUNTRIES HOLD POOR PEOPLE BACK?

The world's developed countries have plenty of wealth and resources. So why are so many of their people poor? Are the poor being held back by lack of opportunity?

Spanish teenagers work at their school computers. Most people in rich countries take easy access to facilities like these for granted.

Excuses and equality

Some people in wealthy nations say that their country's poor should stop making excuses. They believe that poor people have similar opportunities to the rest of the population. Genevieve, a 14-year-old girl from Toulouse, France, holds this view:

❝ I live in a country where by law every child goes to free schools. There are free libraries and people are helped when they cannot afford basic items. Many people have been born poor in France but have improved their lives because our country has given them plenty of chances to improve. ❞

Unequal struggle

The United Nations Children's Fund (UNICEF) reported in 2005 that 40–50 million children in the world's wealthiest countries will grow up poor. Will they be denied the chances that others get in life? Jenz, aged 14, comes from a poor family in Prenzlau, Germany. He feels that the system is against him:

❝ I share a tiny bedroom with my brother. The door only half opens before it hits our beds. There is nowhere for me to do my homework and we don't have a PC like all the other kids in my class have, so I struggle. At school, teachers suggest extra books and visits but my family cannot afford them. How can I compete with others? ❞

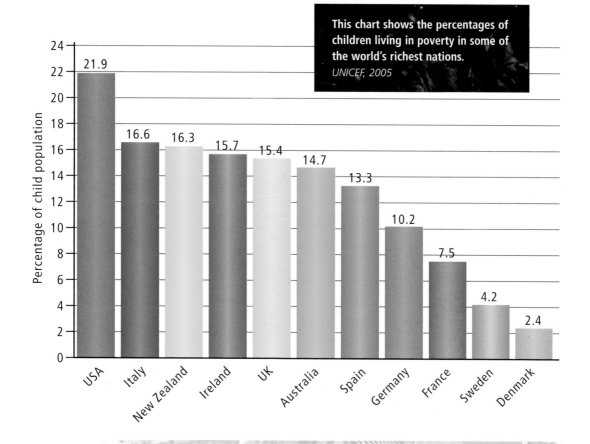

This chart shows the percentages of children living in poverty in some of the world's richest nations.
UNICEF, 2005

Percentage of child population

USA	21.9
Italy	16.6
New Zealand	16.3
Ireland	15.7
UK	15.4
Australia	14.7
Spain	13.3
Germany	10.2
France	7.5
Sweden	4.2
Denmark	2.4

"Most of the men in Easterhouse [Glasgow] hadn't had a job in 20 years. They were dispirited, depressed, often alcoholic. Their self-esteem had gone. Emotionally and mentally they were far worse off than the poor where we worked in India."

Founder of ACCORD charity, Mari Marcel-Thekaekara, on visiting a poor part of Glasgow, Scotland, in 1999.

SHOULD THE POOR HELP THEMSELVES MORE?

Few people become poor through their own choice. But do they need to stay poor? Could they find more ways to pull themselves out of poverty?

These children work hard all day on farms in Cheeri, India. Yet they still attend a school at night, lit by solar powered lanterns.

Taking every chance

Many poor people have no access to transport, electricity, books or schooling. Yet this doesn't stop them taking every chance they can to improve their lives. Felix, who is 15, works long, exhausting days in a factory in Guatemala. But he still manages to study to become a mechanic:

❝ It's an insult to say we poor are lazy. Every day, I work for eight or ten hours, fetch water from the well 30 minutes away and look after my younger sisters. Still, I walk an hour each way to night class and study with a candle as we have no electricity. Give poor people a chance and they will take it. ❞

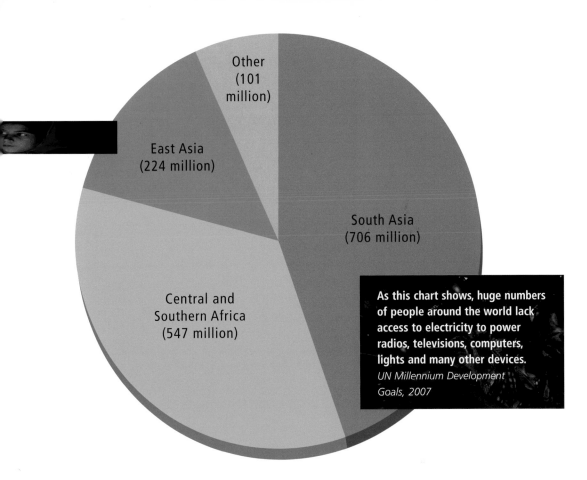

Other
(101 million)

East Asia
(224 million)

South Asia
(706 million)

Central and
Southern Africa
(547 million)

As this chart shows, huge numbers of people around the world lack access to electricity to power radios, televisions, computers, lights and many other devices.
UN Millennium Development Goals, 2007

Missing opportunities

Not all poor people take advantage of opportunities when they are made available. A volunteer working to help the poor in Manila, the Philippines, despairs. She says that the poor do not want her help at training classes, called seminars:

“ They do not understand... they do not want to understand the issues tackled in the seminars. No one asks questions; they do not like to think. They do not want to meddle nor be bothered by others because they have so much work to do. There is no participation... for the development of everyone. ”

"Of course, circumstances – where you are born, your neighbourhood, your school and the choices your parents make – have a huge impact. But social problems [such as poverty] are often the consequence of the choices people make."

David Cameron MP, leader of the UK Conservative Party, 2008.

SHOULDN'T POOR PEOPLE HAVE FEWER CHILDREN?

The world's poorest people often have the largest families.

Is this keeping them poor or helping them to survive?

Limiting family size

Rwanda's population has grown by 400 per cent in the past 50 years. In 2006, women in Rwanda gave birth to an average of six children each. Since then, the government has announced laws to limit families to no more than three children. Jay, an aid worker in Butare, Rwanda, thinks this makes sense:

❝ There is already hardly any space for these growing families to grow food to feed themselves, and with each generation the family plot is further divided... The government here sees a huge problem in the near future that could affect the welfare of the entire country. ❞

This large family from the tiny nation of Burundi is typical of many across Africa. Would their lives be any easier if they had fewer children?

Family survival

Many poor people have large families for a chilling reason – not all of their children will reach adulthood. Children are often needed to care for sick relatives, help with farm work or earn money so the family can survive. Mtembi, from the Central African Republic, says:

❝ I think of my family as blessed. We have had eight children and only two have died. Others in the village have not been so lucky – another family has lost five of their seven children. Our land is poor. Without my children's help to farm it, I think we would all perish. ❞

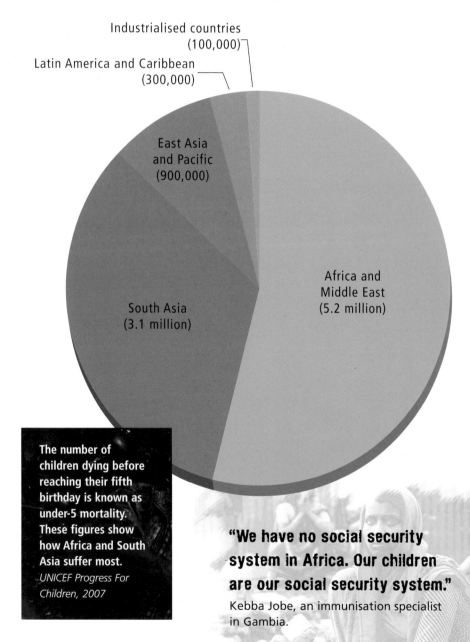

Industrialised countries
(100,000)

Latin America and Caribbean
(300,000)

East Asia
and Pacific
(900,000)

South Asia
(3.1 million)

Africa and
Middle East
(5.2 million)

The number of children dying before reaching their fifth birthday is known as under-5 mortality. These figures show how Africa and South Asia suffer most.
UNICEF Progress For Children, 2007

"We have no social security system in Africa. Our children are our social security system."
Kebba Jobe, an immunisation specialist in Gambia.

IS POVERTY INEVITABLE?

The worlds of business and politics today create wealth for some but lives of poverty for others. Can a balance be found, or is the problem too complex to be solved?

This photo of Sao Paulo, Brazil reveals a huge gap between rich and poor. While hi-tech skyscrapers tower in the distance, poverty in this shanty town on the city outskirts is severe.

No end in sight?

It is easy to think that there will always be people who suffer poverty while others lead prosperous lives. Carol is a 13-year-old from Manitoba in Canada. She cannot see an end in sight:

" You cannot stop poverty from happening. There have always been rich people and rich countries and they will always use their wealth and power to stay rich and keep others poor. Everything's stacked against the poor. "

Schemes like Fair Trade aim to tackle poverty by helping small farmers, like this Nicaraguan coffee grower, to get a better price for their crops. Fair Trade schemes also fund community projects such as schools.

Ending absolute poverty

Some people believe that there are enough resources in the world to wipe out absolute poverty. German development minister, Heidemarie Wieczorek-Zeul feels that spending less on weapons and the military might be the answer:

❝ It would only cost US$20 a head for each man, woman and child living in the world today to achieve all the UN Millennium Goals [including halving absolute poverty by 2015 – see page 41]. Current spending on arms is US$187 a head in real terms. ❞

"Like slavery and apartheid, poverty is not natural. It is man–made and it can be overcome and eradicated by the actions of human beings."
Nelson Mandela, 2005.

CAN FOREIGN AID ATTACK POVERTY?

Foreign aid is when countries or organisations provide help to other, usually poorer, nations. Aid comes in many forms, from projects to build clean water supplies to loans of money or free healthcare. Can aid reduce poverty?

Helping the poorest

Some aid has allowed important long-term schemes to flourish. These provide help and hope to some of the world's poorest people. Moni, a 12-year-old homeless girl from the slums of Santos in Brazil, has benefited:

❝ I was hungry, ill and had nowhere to live. I was close to death and then I was rescued. A new centre opened for homeless children. I was taken in and given food and medicine. Now, I am studying hard. When I grow up, I want to help others just like people have helped me. ❞

Foreign-funded projects, such as this homeless centre in Brazil, can offer the very poor a brand new start in life.

"Sound economic policies, not aid, have lifted millions of Asians out of poverty."
Swedish economist, Fredrik Erixon, 2005.

Refugees in the war-torn region of Darfur, Sudan rely heavily on foreign aid. But does this help to solve core issues such as conflict and poverty in the region?

It's not enough

Not all aid helps the poor – it may be misused or wasted. In some cases, donating countries insist on the money being used in a certain way, putting their own interests first. Even when aid works, some critics argue that it is not enough. Peter Lilley, a senior member of the UK Conservative Party, argues:

❝ Even if the rich countries fulfil their pledges to increase aid, the total amount will still be inadequate to finance all the health, education, nutrition, water and sanitation that people living on the edge of survival need. Above all, they [the poor countries] need economic growth to boost their incomes. ❞

SHOULDN'T WE HELP THOSE AT HOME RATHER THAN ABROAD?

Individuals and governments can donate money to organisations that fight poverty. Should we focus on helping the poor in our own country, or do other people need our help more?

Charity begins at home

Many people feel that governments should concentrate on looking after their own population before others. Paul, a 14-year-old from Chicago, USA, thinks that problems at home should be a priority:

" Our government is elected to look after us, not people in other countries. It's ridiculous. We have enough poor people in our own country to worry about. And we've got plenty of other problems like drugs and crime to deal with. Other countries have got themselves into their mess – they should get themselves out of it. Would they all help us if we were in trouble? I doubt it. "

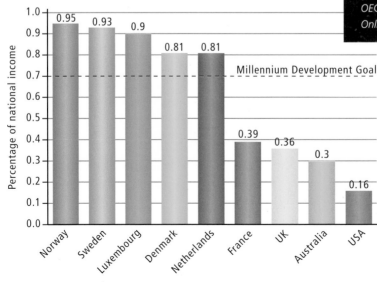

POOR IN THE USA

33% of children in the USA live in families where no parent has full-time, year-round employment.

22% of people aged 18–24 in the USA are in poverty.

8% of teens in the USA are not attending school and not working.

Kids Count, Data Center, 2006

This graph shows the percentage of national income that countries spend on foreign aid. The target set by the Millennium Development Goals (see page 41) is 0.7%.
OECD Development Statistics Online, 2008

Millennium Development Goal

Percentage of national income

Norway	0.95
Sweden	0.93
Luxembourg	0.9
Denmark	0.81
Netherlands	0.81
France	0.39
UK	0.36
Australia	0.3
USA	0.16

Helping those most in need

Other people believe that we live in a global community with a responsibility for all. They say we should help those who are in most desperate need, regardless of where they live. Lisa, a young worker from the UK, explains:

" I try to help as much as I can. I donate money every month to two Third World charities, and I also give extra at times of real crisis (droughts, floods, earthquakes). I don't earn a lot, but I earn much, much more than the people in these countries. We need to stop thinking about ourselves so much, and start giving to others. "

Some 250,000 people march through Edinburgh, Scotland as part of Make Poverty History, 2005. This massive campaign aimed to persuade the richest countries of the world to help the poorest.

IS CHARITY THE ANSWER?

There are hundreds of different charities and other groups acting to help poor people around the world today. They raise vast amounts of money – so why isn't poverty disappearing?

Short-term solution

Some people feel that charity offers only short-term fixes. Bangladesh economist, Muhammad Yunus is one of them. He won the 2006 Nobel Peace Prize for his work in developing microcredit – a system of lending small sums of money to people too poor to get bank loans. He firmly believes that:

❝ People can change their own lives, provided they have the right kind of institutional support. They're not asking for charity, charity is no solution to poverty. Poverty can be overcome by the creation of opportunities like everybody else has... so that they can change their lives. ❞

Muhammad Yunus (right) founded the Grameen Bank, which offers small microcredit loans to millions of poor Bangladeshis. It enabled these women to set up a mobile phone business and earn enough to pay back the loan.

"Microcredit stands as one of the most promising and cost-effective tools in the fight against global poverty."
Jonathan Morduch, Chairperson of the UN Expert Group on Poverty Statistics.

"As each day begins and ends, I don't tire of thanking God for your infinite kindness in helping our children so the light of hope in their lives will never be extinguished."

Brother Alirio Henao thanks the Bolivian Charity Foundation for funds to run homes for handicapped children abandoned by their families.

Women in Mali collect fresh water from a tap funded by the charity Wateraid. Before the tap was in place, they had to drink poor quality water from deep, dirty wells.

Success after success

Charity may not be able to solve every aspect of poverty. But many charity projects have had great success in lifting people out of desperate situations. Chaca is 11 and lives in one of the poorest parts of Peru. He and his family can look forward to the future thanks to two different charity schemes:

❝ Charity people came and changed our lives. They gave us yucca and other crop seeds, which grow so well that we have spare food to sell at market. Other charity people came and built a school. I am now learning to read and write. It is exciting. Our lives are better. ❞

WON'T GLOBALISATION SOLVE POVERTY?

In the past 20 years, the rise of the Internet, global communications and cheaper transport links has allowed businesses to operate all over the world. Can this so-called globalisation help large numbers of the world's poor?

New jobs, new hope

Globalisation has already benefited many people. Some businesses in poorer countries have been able to sell their goods abroad for the first time. In addition, many giant companies have moved jobs to poorer countries where they can pay workers less. Some people say this exploits the poor. Indira, who works in an international call centre in Bangalore, India, disagrees:

" I'm not exploited, I'm the least poor I've ever been! And my taxes and all the other taxes paid by people who work at the call centre can go to help other Indians. I receive twice as much pay working here – my life has been transformed. "

"[Global companies] spread wealth, work, technologies that raise living standards and better ways of doing business. That's why so many developing countries are competing fiercely to attract their investment."

Richard D McCormick, president of the International Chamber of Commerce, 2002.

More than a million people now work in telephone call centres in Indian cities, dealing with customers from overseas.

"Some 2 billion people have gained little or nothing from globalisation. Many of them may never have made a telephone call, let alone used the Internet."

Rob Bowden, author of *World Poverty*.

Indonesians in Jakarta protest against the World Trade Organisation in 2008. Millions of people worldwide believe that globalisation is increasing not decreasing poverty.

Unequal and unfair

Critics of globalisation point out that local businesses in poor countries are often forced to close because they cannot compete with giant companies. They also insist that big businesses will keep moving jobs to wherever is cheapest, forgetting the damage this may leave behind. Manna worked in a clothing factory in Namibia:

We did the work here, we sweated and toiled. But all the profits leave our country and go back to the rich and powerful people who own the big companies. Now, they are going to close the factory down here. This will cause misery and poverty.

CAN WELFARE KEEP PEOPLE IN POVERTY?

Governments spend large sums of money on welfare, or social security, to help people who cannot support themselves. Schemes include benefits to the unemployed, single mothers and old or sick people. Is this money well spent?

Unemployed people queue for benefit applications at a centre in Berlin, Germany. In 2008, Germany had almost 4 million people out of work.

A welfare trap?

Some people feel that generous welfare is unfair. They complain that it dumps high taxes on workers and does not encourage others to help themselves. People may become dependent on benefits rather than finding work. This 'welfare trap' is something that Jenny in Bolton, UK, has witnessed:

❝ My sister's 18 and a poor single parent. But she can earn the same on the social [welfare] as she can working, and all without lifting a finger. She says there's no point in her working, but I think that means she'll always stay poor and be on the social. ❞

"Those who remain on welfare [need] this clear message: If you are able to work or train, you must work or train."
George W Bush, 2000.

While the benefit system is available as back-up, employment services also help people to find work and apply for jobs.

Safety and support

For many people who fall on hard times, welfare acts as a crucial safety net. It offers support to those who want to find work and rebuild their lives. This was the case for Hakan's family when they moved from Turkey to Germany:

" When we arrived in Frankfurt, we needed help to get going. Welfare gave us housing and my parents language and business training. Now, my family run a shop and we are okay. Germany is a powerful and rich nation. It can afford to help us and other poor people at least until we get on our feet. "

COULD RICH PEOPLE DO MORE?

While millions of people struggle in poverty, there are many wealthy individuals in the world. Some already give generously and work hard to fight poverty. Could they and others do more?

Giving generously

Microsoft founder Bill Gates is one of the world's richest men. He has donated over US$7,000 million to charity, including US$750 million to the GAVI Alliance scheme to protect children from dangerous diseases. Gates said of the scheme:

❝ Is there a chance to make a difference? I think so. I think, within a decade, we'll be able to say because of this work there are millions of children alive who wouldn't have been here otherwise. It's an incredible thing, really. ❞

Anita Roddick, who set up The Body Shop, gave away most of her fortune to charities. She said:

❝ I've got everything I want. What do you do with the excess? I think the rich have to look after the poor. ❞

Billionaire Bill Gates helps to distribute a polio vaccine in India. With Gates' financial support, GAVI has already prevented an estimated 2.9 million deaths from disease in the future.

"The world's richest 500 individuals have a combined income greater than that of the poorest 416 million."
UN Human Development Report, 2005.

A Russian woman tries on expensive fur coats at the Millionaire Fair in Moscow. Do wealthy people have a right to spend their own money selfishly?

More than money

Many rich people have worked very hard and taken large risks to become wealthy. Some feel that they do enough in employing people, paying taxes and making donations to charities. Multi-millionaire George Soros believes that giving money is not the only solution to poverty:

❝ Most of the poverty and misery in the world is due to bad government, lack of democracy, weak states, internal strife, and so on. ❞

As well as giving money to fight poverty, should rich people use their power to try to influence businesses and governments?

MILLIONAIRES AND GIVING

Number of US dollar millionaires (2005):	8,700,000
Number of US dollar millionaires (2006):	9,500,000
Estimated total donations to charity by millionaires:	US$285,000,000,000

11th World Wealth Report, 2007

IS THERE HOPE FOR THE FUTURE?

Poverty still rages around the world, but more and more people are recognising the damage that it does. With increasing donations, campaigns and other help for the poor, is there real hope for the future?

Changing the world

Charities, aid and government schemes are saving poor people's lives and decreasing the numbers in poverty. Many poor communities are getting long-term help through education and new business schemes. Melita's village in Honduras has been transformed:

❝ Most of the adults in our village could not read or write, so we could not fight for our land rights or ask for help. Aid workers have set up an adult school and helped our village form a weaving business. We face a better future now. ❞

This Peruvian woman is part of a textiles weaving association that supports over 200 members. The scheme enables people to sell their goods for a fair price, helping to reduce poverty.

So much more to do

Despite some success, vast amounts still need to be done if poverty is to be beaten. Sir Bob Geldof is one campaigner who believes that poverty remains the biggest challenge of the twenty-first century. He recognises the many other problems that stem from people being poor:

" We're looking at the singular condition of poverty. All the other individual problems spring from that condition... doesn't matter if it's death, aid, trade, AIDS, famine, instability, governance, corruption or war. "

Two street children from Thailand sniff glue out of plastic bags. They are among many thousands of desperately poor people who can currently only hope for a better life.

MILLENNIUM GOALS

In 2000, 189 nations signed an agreement called the UN Millennium Development Goals. These are 8 major targets to improve the lives of the world's poor by 2015. At the end of 2007:

● 58 nations were on target to halve extreme poverty by 2015.

● Only 28 of 86 nations were on target to get all of their children into primary schools.

● 51 developing nations were on track to deliver basic sanitation to all of their people.

UNICEF, December 2007

TIMELINE

1601 Poor Laws in England make areas of the country known as church parishes responsible for helping the poor.

1804 The world human population is around 1 billion.

1842 An American doctor, John H Griscom, begins writing *The Sanitary Condition of the Laboring Population of New York City*, one of the first reports to link poverty and disease.

1927 The world population reaches 2 billion.

1929 The Wall Street Crash sees economies collapse and the Great Depression occurs, creating much poverty throughout the world in the 1930s.

1935 A Social Security Act is passed in the USA, providing major welfare programmes for the American poor.

1942 The Oxford Committee for Famine Relief is formed. It later becomes Oxfam, a charity that tackles poverty all over the world.

1945 The World Bank is established. It soon becomes the world's biggest development organisation, providing loans to developing countries.

1945 The United Nations Charter is signed, with a view to international co-operation in achieving peace and solving problems including poverty.

1957 The Gold Coast becomes Ghana, the first independent black country in Africa.

1961 The world population reaches 3 billion.

1961 The charity War on Want first raises concerns about debt in poorer nations and warns it will be a major issue in the future.

1964 The Child Poverty Action Group, a charity committed to ending child and family poverty in the UK, is founded.

1974 The world population reaches 4 billion.

1976 Muhammad Yunus begins offering microcredit loans to poor Bangladeshis.

1982–1983   Mexico does not repay its debts to other nations. This starts a major crisis in loans and debt.

1985   Live Aid concerts are staged in London, UK and Philadelphia, USA, raising millions to help famine victims in Africa.

1987   The world population reaches 5 billion.

1990   The All African Council of Churches calls for a Year of Jubilee to cancel Africa's debts.

1990   The absolute poverty line is defined at US$1 a day for the first time by the World Bank in its World Development Report.

1991   The World Wide Web is created, enabling instant communications and interaction between communities around the planet.

1996   The Heavily Indebted Poor Countries (HIPC) initiative is set up to help poor countries with huge debts.

1999   The world population reaches 6 billion.

2000   A world total of 34 million people are now infected with HIV/AIDS, over 23 million of them in Africa.

2000   The Jubilee Campaign highlights the massive debts that face many poorer nations.

2002   An African conference estimates that corruption costs African nations over US$140 billion per year.

2005   A series of concerts, called Live 8, are held in the G8 nations and South Africa to coincide with the G8 Conference of the world's richest nations and raise awareness about global poverty.

2007   G8 leaders pledge approximately US$60 billion in aid to Africa.

2015   This is the target date for nations to reach their Millennium Development Goals to slash poverty and improve the health and lives of many of the world's poor.

GLOSSARY

benefits Social security payments made to people by a government.

billion One thousand million.

birth control Methods to prevent unwanted pregnancies.

developed nations Wealthy nations like the USA, UK and most of western Europe, with large industries and relatively high average income per member of population.

developing nations Nations seeking to build their industries and wealth, who tend to be poorer and contain many poor people.

drought A very long period of extremely dry weather, causing water shortages and crop failures.

economy The goods, services and wealth produced by a society.

exploit To take advantage of people or a situation, sometimes illegally, for one's own gain.

famine Drastic hunger or starvation due to long-term shortages of food.

G8 Short for group of 8, a group of eight of the world's richest countries: Canada, France, Germany, Italy, Japan, Russia, UK, USA.

gross domestic product (GDP) A way of measuring a country's economic wealth. It is the total value of all goods and services produced by a country in a year.

human rights The basic rights of all people such as the right to free speech, shelter and food.

illegal Against the laws of a country or local area.

malnourished Weak and in bad health because of a lack of food or lack of healthy food.

Millennium Development Goals Anti-poverty targets adopted in 2000 by all the countries that are members of the United Nations. Each country has until 2015 to meet them.

resources Goods, raw materials, money and services used by people to achieve a goal.

rural Describing an area or place in the countryside, away from towns and cities.

sanitation The safe collection and disposal of sewage and other waste.

squatter A person who settles in a house or on land that they have no legal right to.

UNICEF Part of the United Nations, responsible for children's health, education and wellbeing.

United Nations (UN) An international organisation with over 190 member countries, which was formed in 1945 to promote world peace, good health and economic development.

vulnerable Especially at risk.

welfare A system of services and money provided by governments to help their country's poor people.

World Bank An international bank that lends money to countries for development programmes.

RESOURCES

Books

World Poverty (Just The Facts) by Rob Bowden (Harcourt Education, 2002)

A Kids' Guide to Hunger & Homelessness: How to Take Action! by Cathryn Berger Kaye (Free Spirit Publishing, 2007)

Poverty by Teresa Garlake (Wayland, 1999)

Poverty (Planet Under Pressure) by Paul Mason (Heinemann Library, 2006)

Websites

http://www.alertnet.org/topkillerdiseases.htm
This web page gives facts and figures on the diseases that most threaten the world's poor.

http://www.jubileedebtcampaign.org.uk
The website of a campaign group that wants to see more debt removed from poor countries.

http://www.un.org/millenniumgoals/pdf/mdg2007.pdf
A free-to-read report on the Millennium Development Goals and the progress made so far.

http://www.globalempowerment.org/Policy Advocacy/pahome2.5.nsf/geurls!OpenForm
A large list of links to websites dealing with poverty, development and aid.

http://www.makepovertyhistory.org
The official website of the anti-poverty campaign has many useful fact files and case studies.

INDEX